How to Make Huge Cash with Section 8 Rentals the Landlord Handbook

ERNIE BRAVEBOY

Copyright © 2012 Ernie Braveboy

This document is geared towards providing exact and reliable information in regards to the topic and issue covered. The publication is sold with the idea that the publisher is not required to render accounting, officially permitted, or otherwise, qualified services. If advice is necessary, legal or professional, a practiced individual in the profession should be ordered.
- From a Declaration of Principles which was accepted and approved equally by a Committee of the American Bar Association and a Committee of Publishers and Associations.
In no way is it legal to reproduce, duplicate, or transmit any part of this document in either electronic means or in printed format. Recording of this publication is strictly prohibited and any storage of this document is not allowed unless with written permission from the publisher. All rights reserved.
The information provided herein is stated to be truthful and consistent, in that any liability, in terms of inattention or otherwise, by any usage or abuse of any policies, processes, or directions contained within is the solitary and utter responsibility of the recipient reader. Under no circumstances will any legal responsibility or blame be held against the publisher for any reparation, damages, or monetary loss due to the information herein, either directly or indirectly.
Respective authors own all copyrights not held by the publisher.
The information herein is offered for informational purposes solely, and is universal as so. The presentation of the information is without contract or any type of guarantee assurance.
The trademarks that are used are without any consent, and the publication of the trademark is without permission or backing by the trademark owner. All trademarks and brands within this book are for clarifying purposes only and are the owned by the owners themselves, not affiliated with this document.

ISBN: 9781549657641

CONTENTS

Introduction 1

Introduction to the Section 8 Housing Program 3

    Why You Should Become a Section 8 Landlord 4

The Responsibilities of All Parties under the Section 8 Housing Program ... 7

    The Landlord 7

    The Tenant 9

Registration and Qualification 11

    Common Reasons Why the Housing Authority Disqualifies Landlords 11

Checklist to Help You Prepare for the Inspection Process 15

How to Apply as a Section 8 Landlord 20

    Disputing Housing Authority Decisions 21

Fixing Rent and Utility Fees 23

Screening Tenants 27

    Why Should You Screen Section 8 Tenants? 27

    So How Do You Screen Section 8 Housing Tenants? 28

    Tenancy Approval 31

    Drafting Your Lease Agreement 32

    Handling Security Deposit Issues for Section 8 Properties 33

Attracting Tenants to Your Section 8 Property 35

Maintaining and Managing Your Property 40

ERNIE BRAVEBOY

Using a Property Manager- Questions to Ask 41

Tips For Handling Dirty Tenants 45

Increasing Your Rent 47

Evicting Tenants and Termination of Assistance to the Tenant 49

Conclusion 52

Introduction

I want to thank you and congratulate you for buying the book, *"How to Make Huge Cash with Section 8 Rentals- the Landlord Handbook"*.

This book has lots of actionable information on how to make lots of cash with section 8 rentals.

Real estate is one of the most lucrative forms of businesses and investments anywhere in the world because people would always need a roof over their heads i.e. with or without recession.

While there are many ways to make money in real estate, rental properties are a cut above the rest especially owing to the fact that with rental properties, income is somewhat stable compared to other investment options. I know there are times when property might be vacant and other times when tenants come up with all manner of excuses not to pay rent on time. This can definitely mess up your income projections and mess up with your financial plans.

The question you might be asking is; is there any way you can mitigate that? Well, you can; if stability is one of the things you are looking for as you invest in rental property, perhaps the one thing you should be thinking of is venturing into section 8 rental business. The section 8 housing scheme is one of the ways that real estate investors can earn good money on their properties. It is unfortunate that many real estate owners are either unaware that these opportunities exist, or have no clear idea on how to become a part of this business.

In fact, many landlords who have tried to join this business in the past also had their applications rejected due to their inability fulfill the requirements of the program. You don't have to go through the same trouble, as this book breaks down what the section 8 housing program entails, and shows every landlord interested in the section 8 program, how to qualify for the program, select the right tenants, set the best rent rates, and make impressive income from the Section 8 Housing Program. Let's begin.

Thanks again for buying this book. I hope you enjoy it!

INTRODUCTION TO THE SECTION 8 HOUSING PROGRAM

Before we discuss the specifics of how to make the most use of section 8 rentals to derive the full benefits of the program, let's start by building a strong understanding of the section 8 housing program.

Introduction to the Section 8 Housing Program

The Section 8 Housing Program is one of the many initiatives taken by the government to ensure that low-income families in the country never have to go homeless.

It is similar to the food voucher program and it actually works on a voucher system, only that this time, it involves housing provision and not food.

The United States Department of Housing and Urban Development funds the Section 8 Housing Program but the program is administered by the Housing Authority as a means of providing rental assistance to low-income families.

The Housing Authority issues a voucher, which covers a fixed amount of the monthly rent to the tenant. The tenant is be required to pay between 28% - 40% of their monthly income, while the Housing Authority covers the rest. The Section 8 Housing Voucher covers for rent, as well as Utilities.

While the program is great for low-income families on one side, the other side of the coin also has beneficiaries i.e. landlords. To help you understand just why you should take action now, let's discuss some compelling reasons why you should become a section 8 landlord.

Why You Should Become a Section 8 Landlord

You can derive many benefits when you become a Section 8 Landlord. For starters, it is one of the most lucrative ways to make income from your properties because it is a form of partnership between you, the section 8 Landlord, and the Government. Let's discuss the benefits in detail:

- **Guaranteed Timely Payments**: You would not have to go chasing tenants to pay rent any longer.

The Section 8 Housing Voucher program ensures that you get monthly payments on your properties in a timely fashion.

Even if your tenant suffers a reduction in their income, it doesn't affect monthly payments as the Housing Authority already has a way of responding to such situations.

What they usually do is to reduce the portion of rent that the tenant is required to pay, and then increase the portion for the tenants so that at the end of the day, you get your rent payments regardless of your tenant's economic situation.

- **Minimal Paperwork**: Many Landlords scamper away when they hear of the Section 8 Voucher Program, due to the stereotype that anything that involves the government would have to involve a lot of paperwork, bureaucracy, and bottlenecks.

However, I can authoritatively inform you that the Section 8 Housing Program is different.

The Housing Authority wants to ensure that as many Landlords as possible, participate in the program so that there would always be houses for low-income tenants to occupy, so they reduce the paperwork involved such that, the Landlord is responsible for screening, and selecting tenants, and handles his own lease agreement.

All that is left for the Housing Authority to do is to inspect the house, give their nod, and start paying you their own portion of the income.

- **Property Maintenance**: If you want your house to always be in a good shape for a very long period, becoming a section 8 Landlord will help you achieve this.

The Housing Authority carries out regular inspections on properties enrolled in the program, so you have no other choice than to ensure that your properties are properly maintained at all times.

- **Resale Value**: From experience, joining the Section 8 Housing Program helps to increase the resale value of your property due to the fact that you always have to carry out maintenance and repairs for inspection and if you decide to sell your property in the future, it would be in a very good shape, and attract a high value.

- **Easy to Get Tenants:** You don't necessarily have to go through the stress with property agents to fill up your house. There is an online listing tool provided by the Housing Authority to help low-income families enrolled in the program find housing space by listing all the vacant houses available.

Therefore, it's always easy to get people to fill up your space without having to pay commission to your agents.

With the information on how you stand to gain by becoming a section 8 rental landlord in mind, let's now demystify what your role will be as a section 8 rental landlord.

THE RESPONSIBILITIES OF ALL PARTIES

UNDER THE SECTION 8 HOUSING PROGRAM

The Landlord

The Section 8 Program is a three-way partnership between the Landlord, the Tenant and the Housing Authority.

To help you understand how the program works, let's break down the responsibilities of each of the parties to the contract, starting with the Landlord.

1. As the Landlord, it is your responsibility to ensure that your housing units and premises are always maintained, and in accordance with the standards of the Housing Authority.

Some tenants may be destructive or careless with your property but it remains your responsibility to ensure that these damages are fixed promptly, before inspection days to avoid disqualification.

You might have to add a surcharge to your rent for maintenance, but you have to be careful when doing this

because the Housing Authority expects that rents charged by Landlords enrolled in the program, should not exceed the rents of any other houses within the area.
2. It is also your responsibility to ensure that only the families listed on your lease agreement occupies the building. Section 8 tenants are not allowed to sublet their properties to other people, and it is your responsibility as the landlord to enforce this.
3. You must also fix a fair price as rent on your property at all times. The total amount for rent and utilities must not exceed those of other properties in the neighborhood.
4. You cannot sell, lease out, or enter into an agreement with any other party for the property, while still under the Section 8 Contract.
5. Another one of your responsibilities as a Landlord is to ensure that tenants who are enrolled under the program, do not have any ownership interests or investments in the properties that they are occupying. So no fraudulent moves or gimmicks by tenants who are trying to play a fast one of the government and take advantage of the Section 8 Housing System.
6. You cannot rent out your property to any of your family members, or anybody that is directly related to you whether they qualify for the Vouchers or not.

Sorry, but your family members would have to look for another enrolled property to occupy.

However, if that family member is disabled, or in some cases, if you, the Landlord does not reside in that building, the Housing Authority may allow you to rent out some units to your relatives.
7. It is also your responsibility to ensure that all the terms of lease are adhered to by the tenants. You

have to ensure that illegal activities such as illegal drug trafficking, gambling and any other criminal activity are not carried out within the units.
8. Lastly, it is your responsibility to decide on the utilities the tenant would be responsible for, and those that would be included in the rent.

Next, we will learn about the role of the tenant.

The Tenant

The second party to the contract is the tenant. There are responsibilities that rest on beneficiaries of Section 8 Housing Vouchers and some of them include:
1. The house must be used as their principal place of residence. Tenants are not allowed to rent houses as additional living spaces, holiday homes or give it outs to other people. Anybody who is participating in the Section 8 program as a beneficiary must be a genuine, low-income individual who needs the house as a primary living space.
2. Tenants must ensure that they pay up their portion of the rent. After the Housing Authority pays its own portion, the tenant must ensure that they pay their own portion as well.
3. Tenants are not allowed to sublet the housing units.
4. Tenants are expected to supply any information required by the Housing Authority for determining whether they are eligible for the program or otherwise.
5. The tenants are expected to inform the Housing Authority in writing, whenever they would be away from the property for extended periods.
6. Whenever the tenant's economic situation changes, the tenant is also expected to inform the Housing Authority

for reexamination purposes.
7. If the tenant has to move out of the property, it is their duty to inform both the landlord and the Housing Authority prior to the move.
8. The tenant must make the house available for regular inspection by the housing unit.
9. If the tenant needs to add an extra family member as occupant of the property, they have to receive approval from the Housing Authority.
10. If the landlord ever issues an eviction notice to the tenant, the tenant has to make a copy of the eviction notice available to the Housing Authority.

Basically, beneficiaries of the Section 8 Housing Program must always ensure that the units are never used for any illegal dealings, and they stay true to the purpose behind the program which is to provide housing assistance to underprivileged families.

The next chapter contains information about how to register, pass the approval and qualification process, to become a Section 8 landlord.

REGISTRATION AND QUALIFICATION

The first step involved in becoming a Section 8 landlord is to pass the approval and qualification process. Many landlords often have their applications rejected because they are unable to pass this stage. If you follow the steps outlined in this chapter however, you will not have a problem getting your applications approved.

Before we get to the application process, let's first understand why applications are rejected.

Common Reasons Why the Housing Authority Disqualifies Landlords

Before your property can be approved to be enrolled in the program, a visit is made to the property to inspect it and ensure that the property meets the standards of the program. Some of the reasons why some properties are disqualified include:

- **Electrical Hazards**: One of the standards of the Housing Authority is that the housing units do not expose the tenants to potential electrical hazards.

Therefore, the electrical outlets and switches in the housing units must be covered by plates that are secured to the walls, and are not cracked. All light fixtures must also be present and properly working, and they must be mounted to the ceilings or walls.

Breaker boxes must not have exposed wires, and they must all have open spaces filled with blank spacers or knockouts.

- **Entry Door Problems**: All doors leading to the units must be able to lock securely. The doors must also have weather-stripping to prevent air penetration.
- **Windows**: If the units have broken window panes, that would lead to automatic disqualification because the windows are expected to be in good condition, unbroken and able to open and lock up easily. Thumbscrews and sticks are not accepted as locking devices for windows.
- **Refrigerator**: The kick plate must be secured at the bottom of the refrigerators, and the rubber gasket must be fixed properly around the doors and be in good condition too.
- **Oven or Range**: The Housing Authority seeks to prevent fire breakouts so they expect that all oven burners be laid flat, and all elements including knobs and dials are working properly. There must also be a filter screen in front of the fan and the oven and range must be properly cleaned.
- **Hot Water Heaters**: Any housing unit with hot water heaters that do not have discharge lines and pressure relief valves that extend to within six inches of the floor, may be disqualified. The discharge tubing must also not be made of PVC. You may use

Copper, Galvanized Steel or CPVC piping.

Make sure there are no exposed wires around your water heaters, or flammable materials stored near the hot water tank too.

- **Heating and Plumbing**: All heating systems must function properly and be able to generate the right amount of heat. All sources of heat must also be clear of items like clothing, furniture and beddings. The furnaces for gas, propane or oil must be regularly serviced, and none of the plumbing fixtures must be leaking.
- **Ventilation**: Bathroom fans must be working properly, and the housing units must be properly ventilated.
- **Flooring**: Any types of flooring and flooring damages that may lead to tripping hazards, may lead to disqualification. Floors with dry rots, or carpets with exposed tacks, may also lead to disqualification.
- **Smoke Detectors**: Landlords are expected to install smoke and carbon monoxide detectors on each floors of the housing unit if not in each apartment and there must also be a tester button attached to it.

If you plan to rent the space out to hearing-impaired persons, the smoke detectors must come with alarms suitable for hearing-impaired persons, and the alarms must be installed in the room that is going to be occupied by them.

- **Paint**: There must be no peeling paints in the interior or exterior areas of the building if the building would be occupied by children.
- **Steps, Decks and Railings**: Stairways must have handrails that run the length of the stairways and must be secured to guarantee adequate safety of the

tenants. The steps, decks and railings must also be free of dry-rot and any other tripping hazards.

These are some of the reasons why homes are disqualified from participating in the Section 8 program.

The Housing Authority conducts inspection as part of the applications' review process. When you apply to join the Section 8 program as a landlord, the Housing Authority will schedule a date to come to your property to inspect it and determine whether it meets its standards and requirements.

Before you start your application process (which we will discuss shortly), I have prepared a checklist for you. This checklist will help you prepare for inspection so that you can be sure of getting a nod from the Housing Authority.

CHECKLIST TO HELP YOU PREPARE FOR THE INSPECTION PROCESS

Entryway
- Check all floor coverings; are they properly secured to the floor?
- Are the carpets tacked down?
- Are the carpets free of any fraying?
- Are the Vinyl securely affixed?

Living Room
- Check all the heat sources; are they all working properly?
- Are all the electrical sources and outlets working and properly wired?
- Are all the covers of the electrical outlets free of cracks and any other damages?
- Are the floor coverings secured to the floor?
- Are the carpets tacked down and free of fraying?
- Are the windows free of molds and mildew?
- Are the carpet hooks properly covered up?

- Are the Vinyl floorings securely fixed?

Bedroom

- Check all the walls of the bedroom- are they in good shape and free of holes?
- Is there at least one outlet and an overhead light in each of the bedrooms?
- Are there any broken door frames you should fix?
- Are there any bad door jambs than need to be replaced?
- Are all the electrical outlets in the bedroom working properly?
- Do you have any three-pronged electrical outlets in the bedrooms; are they properly grounded?
- Do all the bedroom windows have permanent locks that are in good shape? You can have bars or sticks as secondary locks but there must be a permanent lock too.
- Can all the doors close properly?
- Do all the doors have striker plates?
- Are the closet doors in good shape?
- Are the carpets in the bedroom tacked down properly and free of fraying? The carpet hooks are not exposed either?
- Are the Vinyl securely fixed?

Kitchen

- Check the appliances; are they in good working condition? This includes the dishwasher, ovens, refrigerator and stove burners.
- The cabinet edges; do they have smooth edges?
- Are there any cracks or chips on the cabinet doors that need to be fixed?
- Are the cabinet doors properly secured to the wall?

- The refrigerator door; is it in good condition? Are there any cracks or broken seals you need to fix?
- Are the floorings in good shape with no cracks or portions that are not properly secured to the wall?
- Check the range; are the fans and hood light working?
- Is the garbage disposal working?
- Are all wirings hidden and securely installed?
- Are all pipes and plumbing in good condition? Are there any rusts or leaking or molds that need to be taken care of?

The Hallways

- Are there smoke and carbon monoxide detectors on each of the floor levels of the building? Do the detectors have tester buttons that work when pushed?
- Are the carpets free of fraying and properly tacked down with the hooks carefully covered?
- If there are closets in the hallway, are they hung on hinges and on track?

Bathrooms

- Are the bulbs all working and covered up?
- Are the pipes and plumbing all in good condition and free from leakages, rusts and molds?
- Are the towel bars properly secured to the walls?
- Are all the electrical outlets wired correctly, working properly, and rid of any cracked or broken covers?
- Is there a Ground Floor Interrupter (GFI) Outlet for renovated or new outlets?
- Are the sinks, tubs and toilets in good condition?
- Are all the cabinet edges smooth and free of obvious cracks and chips? Are they properly secured to the wall?
- Are the toilets properly secured to the floor and not leaking?

- Are the bath fans in good working condition?
- Are the bath tubs caulked around the wall and sealed at the base?
- Are the bathrooms and toilets mold and mildew free?
- Are there any leaks, chipping paints or moisture problems that need to be fixed?

Hot Water Tanks

- Are the discharge line pipes made of the right material, which is either galvanized steel, CVPC pipe or hard copper?
- Do the hot water tanks have temperature gauges and pressure relief valves?
- Are they properly secured to the walls with a wall bracket?

Electrical System

- Do all circuit breaker boxes have doors and securely fixed to the walls with no spaces in between?
- Are there Ground Fault Interrupter (GFI) outlets and are they working perfectly?

Front and Back Doors

- Are the window panes in excellent condition?
- Are the door jambs in excellent condition?
- Is there weather stripping on all exterior doors?
- Are all the locks and bolts functioning perfectly?

Exterior

- Do all the stairways with four or more stairs have handrails?
- Are the down sprouts and gutters secured to the building structure?
- Are the laundry rooms and other extra areas designed for the tenant's use properly lit up and hazard free?
- Are there any abandoned or broken down vehicles that need to be moved out of the property?
- Do the exterior doors have working lights above them?
- Are there any appliances stored around the yard, or on the porch, which need to be removed?
- Are the exterior areas free of glass, abandoned materials, junk or debris that need to be removed?
- Are all the exterior walls and surfaces in good condition and free from cracked and chirped paint?
- Are all the pillars and support structurally sound?
- Are the exterior doors the only doors that have locks where keys are necessary to unlock them? Bedroom, bathroom and other interior doors should not have keyed entry locks.

With that checklist in mind, let's now move on to discuss how to apply as a section 8 landlord.

HOW TO APPLY AS A SECTION 8 LANDLORD

When you are sure that your housing units meet all the standard requirements, you can now begin the application process.

The steps you need to take include:

- **Contact the Housing Authority**: You should first look for the contact information of the Department of Housing and Urban Development Housing Authority Office in your area. You will need a physical address, a phone number and an email address.

    You can use this portal to figure these out.

- **Inform Them That Your Housing Unit is Available**: You can visit them or call them up to inform them of the availability of your housing unit for enrollment in the program. You will be asked to fill out an application form that provides details about you and the housing unit such as your personal information, the location and type of building, number of housing units, as well as the appliances and facilities available.

After you have applied, the Housing Authority will carry out inspection of the property and if you qualify (And you should, provided that you used the checklist above), your housing unit will be approved for rental for Section 8 tenants.

At this point, you can now start advertising your housing unit for rent. You should understand that the Housing Authority is under no obligation to compel tenants to rent your house. It is up to the tenants to decide whether they want to rent your house or otherwise.

In the next few chapters however, we will learn how to set the right rent and clever marketing skills that would help to ensure that you are never short of tenants to occupy your building. But first, the question you might be having is; so what if your application is rejected; can you dispute the rejection? Well, yes you can. Let's discuss that next.

Disputing Housing Authority Decisions

It is possible for you to dispute the decision of the Housing Authority in cases where your first application is rejected.

The Housing Authority gives you the opportunity to review its decisions, and decide whether they are in accordance with the law or otherwise.

You can ask for a review of the determination with a reference to the specific issue that they want you to fix in writing.

You must then fix the problem, and ask for another inspection from a Section 8 supervisor. A supervisor who was not part of the first inspection is assigned to carry out another inspection, and issue a final determination within 10 days.

The key to making this work is to ensure that you fix all the problems as soon as you receive a copy of their review so that by the time another inspection will be conducted, all the problems would have been fixed.

Next, we will discuss how to fix rent and utility fees for your rental units.

FIXING RENT AND UTILITY FEES

Apart from ensuring that your Housing Unit meets the standards of the housing Authority, you would also have to ensure that your rent is fair enough as this is one of the factors that the Housing Authority will take into consideration before approving tenants who want to rent your space.

The key to earning good income under the Section 8 Housing Program also lies with fixing the right amount as rent rates.

Two major factors determine the rent rates that are fixed for Section 8 Housing Units.

1: Fair Market Rates

The Fair Market Rates refer to the market rates that ought to be charged for a property with a certain number of bedrooms in a specific area in the country.

For instance, there is a fair market rate for three-bedroom homes in Los Angeles, just as there is a fair-market rate for two-bedroom homes in New York.

Market rates for properties cannot be the same all over the country or even in the same state so every year, the Housing Authority determines what would be a Fair

Market Rate for properties in an area based on renter surveys, and it would expect that Landlords do not charge Section 8 tenants above these rates.

The Fair Market rates cover the base rent and essential utilities. Essential utilities include electricity and gas while other utilities like internet, telephone and television are classified as non-essential, and are not included in the fair market rates.

2: Payment Standards

The second factor that goes into determining rental rates for Section 8 Housing Units by the Housing Authority is the payment standards.

It doesn't matter how much you personally think that your property is worth in the open market; the Housing Authority will only pay you based on fair market rates and its payment standards.

Each state, city and county has its own Voucher Payment Standards that it sets and uses every year.

For instance, the Voucher Payment Standards for New York City for the Year 2017 is seen in the table below:

New York City

Housing Voucher Payment Standard

Effective January 1, 2017

Bedroom Size	Studio Unit	1 Bedroom	2 Bedroom	3 Bedroom	4 Bedroom	5 Bedroom	6 Bedroom	7 Bedroom	8 Bedroom

| Payment Standards | $1,460 | $1,533 | $1,768 | $2,270 | $2,448 | $2,816 | $3,183 | $3,550 | $3,917 |

When you are setting your Section 8 Housing rent rates, the first rule is to ensure that the rates do not exceed the fair market value rates and the payment standards otherwise; the Housing Authority might continue to reject applications from tenants wishing to occupy your building, with the excuse that it is too expensive.

You can set your rents considering some of the other factors outlined below but you must always put fair market rates and voucher payments standards at the top of the list when analyzing the factors you would use to determine your rent rates.

- **Location**: You should consider the location of your property. You can charge higher rent rates if your property is located in a highbrow area or a desirable area.
- **Square Footage**: Not all three bedroom-sized homes are created equal. You may have a three-bedroom home that is significantly larger than most three bedroom homes in the market and you deserve to charge higher rates for the extra square footage. Your property may also command higher rent rates if it has more bathrooms.
- **Demand**: Properties with high demand rates can also charge more. If your unit is in an area that is highly competitive in the rent market for instance, your property can command higher rates than those of other properties enrolled in the program.
- **Amenities**: The amenities that you have put into your

units would also determine how much you choose to rent it out. Traditionally, homes with more amenities, command higher rent rates in the property market.

It may take a bit of a trial and error before you can fix the perfect price for your Section 8 rental property but using the tips above, you would be able to make headway. Plus, if you're still finding it difficult to set prices, you can try to find three properties that are similar to yours, and enrolled in the Section 8 program. Find out what their rates are, and set your rates to be the same as theirs, or adjust accordingly if they don't have as much amenities or space as yours.

Next, we will focus on discussing how to screen tenants.

SCREENING TENANTS

I mentioned some of the duties of Section 8 Landlords earlier on, and I mentioned that it is the duty of the landlord to screen tenants before renting the properties to them. The first question you might ask is; why should you screen the tenants anyway? Let's discuss that:

Why Should You Screen Section 8 Tenants?

The fact that the tenant is a Section 8 tenant doesn't necessarily mean that they would be good tenants. There are good Section 8 tenants and there are bad ones just like there are good and bad tenants in any rental market.

It is however your duty as a landlord to conduct all the necessary checks and screening exercises to ensure that you rent out your property to the right tenants because mostly, the Housing Authority is only concerned with ensuring that the property is in good shape and conforms to its standards, and its own portion of the rental fees are paid as and when due.

The question of whether a tenant is good or bad for you is up to you, the Section 8 landlord to answer.

So How Do You Screen Section 8 Housing Tenants?

You have to be very careful here, so that you are not accused of discrimination. It helps to have the same screening guidelines for all applicants, and adopt the same screening process each time you screen tenants.

Develop your screening guidelines, and have them written down so that if you are ever accused of discrimination, you can easily prove your innocence.

The guidelines for screening section 8 tenants are pretty much the same as screening regular tenants. You can use some of the guidelines below:

1. **Determine Eligibility for the Section 8 Housing Program**: You don't want to fall for Section 8 Housing scams so the first thing you have to do is to ensure that the tenant qualifies for the Section 8 program. You can obtain a copy of the eligibility requirements from the Housing Authority after your application is approved.
2. **Ensure that the Tenant is Not Related or Own Interest in Your Property**: As a section 8 Landlord, you have to ensure that the Section 8 tenant has no interests or investments in the property, and is not related to you, the landlord except in cases where the tenant is disabled.
3. **Obtain Financial Information**: You must always remember that the Housing Authority only covers a portion of the rent, and the other portion is covered by the tenant so you still have to carry out all the necessary financial checks to ascertain that the tenant has a regular and steady source of income and has a credit history that you are comfortable with.
4. **Conduct Background Checks:** It is also up to you to ensure that your property is not occupied by

people of questionable character and used for criminal activities so if you feel the need to conduct background checks on potential tenants, you should go for it.
5. **Check with the Last Landlord:** You can ask for details of the name, address and phone numbers of the last landlord of the last home the tenant occupied, from the Housing Authority. You can find out what type of tenant they are, and whether they meet your tenancy standards.
6. **Interview the Tenant**: Don't ever forget to interview your potential tenants before you rent your housing space to them. During the interview process, there are some important questions that you need to ask them:
    - When do you plan to move in? This is very necessary in cases where you have tenants currently occupying the unit, who have signified their intentions to move out of the property. You have to know how much time you have to get the apartment ready for the Section 8 tenant.
    - How much do you earn? You may have requested pay-slips from the tenants during your financial screening process but you must understand that pay-slips are historical documents. The tenant's financial situation may have changed between the time they earned the figures seen in the pay-slip and the time of interview and asking the question specifically, helps to confirm that the tenant can pay their own portion of the rent with ease.
    - Can I ask for references from your employer or former landlords? If the tenant is not a first-time tenant, they should have no problem giving you a

nod to go ahead and ask their former landlord for references.

You may need to ask a former landlord and not the landlord of the house they are currently looking to move out from because if they are moving out of the house due to some dissatisfaction or disagreement with the current landlord, the landlord would obviously jump at the opportunity to leave bad reviews about the tenant. Or to be doubly sure, you can ask for references from the tenant's last two landlords. If none of them has anything nice to say about the tenant, then there is a genuine red flag there.

- Would you consent to a credit and background check? If the tenant doesn't want you to conduct a credit check or a background check, then you already know that they have something unpleasant to hide.
- How many of you will be living in this Apartment? Remember that I mentioned that it is your responsibility to ensure that only the family that rents the house under the Section 8 Program would be allowed to live in the housing units, and it is your duty as the Landlord to enforce this.

This is why you need to know the number of people who would be living in the units before you give out your keys.

These questions will help you decide on the right tenants to give your properties out to and which ones to avoid but when making your decision, you should avoid making a decision during the interview process. Your decision should not only be based on how much of a sweet talker the tenant is, or how innocent they look. You should only make your decision after the interview, and after you have conducted additional checks.

You should also avoid making decisions based on sob stories; you are in this for the money and making the highest amount of profit should be foremost on your mind, except in cases where you just want to be charitable.

At a glance, people you should never rent out your property to (Because most of them make problematic tenants in the future) include:

- People undergoing bankruptcy
- People with prior felony convictions (Within the last 7 years)
- People who have had to be evicted from properties in the past, or had eviction cases filed against them.
- People with bad financial or credit history.
- People with fraudulent or criminal history.

The interview process is not always a one-way thing; however, the tenants may also have a few questions for you:

You are allowed to charge your potential section 8 tenants screening fees but you must ensure that the screening fees are the same amount charged to non-section 8 tenants.

Tenancy Approval

After you have screened your tenants and you have ascertained that they meet your approval, you would have to fill out four forms:

1. Request for Tenancy Approval
2. Section 8 Landlord Certification
3. Request for Tax Identification Number Form
4. Lead Based Paint Form

You and the approved tenant will have to fill out these forms, and submit them to the Housing Authority. The Housing Authority will then review the tenancy request, especially the rent rates, compares it with the fair market rates and payment standards and then schedule a second inspection.

So inspections will be conducted on your property twice; the first time would be when you are applying to enroll as a Section 8 landlord and the second time would be every time a new Section 8 tenant wants to move into one of your housing units.

A few major factors are considered during this second inspection visit.
1. That the rent is reasonable and fair, and the amount the tenant would have to pay, would not exceed 40% of their monthly income.
2. The property meets the Housing Quality Standards, as outlined in the first chapter of this book.

Once the tenant's application to rent your unit is approved by the Housing Authority, the screening process is complete and you can now hand your keys over to them. As you do that, ensure to have the lease agreement ready. Let's discuss how to draft the lease agreement.

Drafting Your Lease Agreement

Another responsibility that rests on you as a Section 8 landlord, is drafting the lease forms and agreements that you would have your tenants sign.

Most states have specific lease agreements that landlords are allowed to give to their tenants. You can print out a copy from here or here.

You should find out what the rules and laws that govern Landlord-Tenant policies are in your star as they still apply to Section 8 landlords and tenants.

You may also have your lawyer draft a lease agreement for you- it's even safer but it's not really necessary if you want to avoid spending too much money but generally, your lease agreement should contain the name of the tenants, the address of the property, the amount charged as rent every month, the term of lease, the amount charged as security deposit, any late fee surcharges, conditions for moving into the property and any other provisions against smoking, keeping pets and using the property's utilities.

The lease agreement should be signed only after you have verbally explained all the terms and conditions, and any implications and penalties to the tenants.

It also helps to have witnesses or lawyers present during the time of signing, in case of legal proceedings in the future.

Next, we will discuss security deposits.

Handling Security Deposit Issues for Section 8 Properties

Section 8 or not, charging security deposit is a very essential aspect of real estate rentals.

You may be lucky to have prim and proper tenants, who would use your property nicely with little or no damages for you to fix but this is hardly the case.

Some tenants will misuse your property, and leave you with many damages to fix and it is a loss to you if you have to spend your own money to fix those damages.

The Section 8 program allows you to charge security deposits on your rental properties.

The Security deposits are fully paid by the tenant and not the Housing Authority, so you must ensure that you collect your security deposit directly from the tenant before or at the point of signing the lease agreement.

If your tenant complains that they are unable to afford

security deposits, it is not a wise decision to let the have the property without paying security deposit. Security deposit is your own insurance against damages to your properties so you have to be strict about it and advise them to reach out to agencies and assistance agencies that can help them pay the security deposits.

The Security deposit you charge them must however, never exceed the maximum state security deposit limit.

In the next chapter, we will discuss how to attract tenants to your property.

ATTRACTING TENANTS TO YOUR SECTION 8 PROPERTY

Just like non-section 8 rental properties, your section 8 properties would not attract tenants all by themselves without you taking some steps to attract the right tenants to your property.

The faster your properties are off the market, and the higher the rate of occupancy of your properties, the more money you stand to earn so it helps to ensure that you employ the necessary marketing skills that would help you keep your Section 8 property off the market at all times, so that you can make profit. Here are some ideas, which will help you to attract tenants with the most ease:

1. **Repairs and Cleaning**: First, you have to look through the house and ensure that all the fixtures, fittings and appliances are in good condition. No tenant wants to rent a house where they have to repair facilities or where necessary facilities are unavailable.

Don't hesitate to spend good money to give your house a facelift because this will help to attract more tenants, command higher rent rates, and improve the resale value of your property whenever you decide to resell.

Before you start listing out the properties too, you should have the properties thoroughly cleaned. A clean house always looks better.

2. **Take Professional Photos**: To attract tenants faster, you may have to list your properties online and that requires that you have professional and attractive photos of the house taken so that prospective tenants would fall in love with the houses even before they schedule an inspection visit.

3. **List your Houses**: Although the Housing Authority has its own directory where it lists vacant section 8 houses, that may not be enough to get you tenants fast. If you want to speed things along, you should list your vacant units in other places as well. Remember that the goal is to attract tenants faster, and to reduce vacancy rates so you have to be proactive.

Some places to list your vacant units include:

- **Newspapers**: You don't have to do this if you're looking for free resources because it costs money but if you can spare some dollars, you can consider paying for newspaper ads for your properties.
- **Put Up Yard Signs**: This is one free method that converts very fast. People in the neighborhood, passersby, and other tenants can see the sign posts and help to spread the word to other people who may be looking for vacant units to rent.

  You should also inform tenants about vacant units and they would help you spread the word for free.

- **Craigslist**: Craigslist has become a favorite place for people to look for almost anything. Put up nice looking photos of your property on Craigslist, indicate that it is a Section 8 property, and word would spread very fast about the vacancy especially if it is an attractive unit.
- **Facebook**: Facebook is a good place to post your vacancies too. Millions of people visit this social media platform every day, and there is no doubt that you can reach many people through this medium free. You can also try other social media platforms like Twitter, Google Hangouts, YouTube and online forums.
- **Churches and Welfare Programs**: These are organizations that often provide assistance to underprivileged individuals and would likely know about a few people who need living spaces so don't hesitate to inform local churches and charity organizations in your area.
- **Other Online Resources:** There are also a couple of other online resources that you can use for listing your Section 8 properties such as Postlets.com, Zillow.com, Trula.com, Hotpads.com, Rent.com, ApartmentGuide.com, Realtor.com, Padmapper.com and YouTube.
- **Use an Agent**: If you don't mind paying a little extra to agents as commission, you may also consider using a property agent. Most of them have skills and techniques that they can use to find tenants faster than landlords, and when you use their services, you may be able to fill up your vacant units faster.
1. **Host an Open House**: When prospective tenants

view your property listing, they will always want an opportunity to take a good look at the property so that they can make final decisions about whether they want to rent the property or not. You can follow these steps below to host a successful open house, especially if you don't plan on using the services of property agents.

- **Choose a Convenient Time and Date**: If you don't really have a lot of time to spare, you can host just one open house on a chosen date or once in a week, on days when you would have some time to free up. You should leave out at least 4-5 hours for the event because you may need a little more or less than that, depending on the number of people who show up for the inspections.
- **Inform Current Tenants and Have Them Vacate the House During the Open House**: It is best to have current tenants/occupants of the units stay away from the property at the time of inspections so you may have to politely inform them, and give them a specific date/time when you plan to host the open day so that they can also prepare themselves to comply accordingly.
- **Advertise and Build Excitement**: A few weeks leading up to the event (1 week is fine), you should start advertising the event on all the platforms that you have listed the vacancies. This gives people enough time to plan to show up at the events. You can also have a sort of pre-registration done, and collect the email addresses and phone numbers of people who are interested in coming for the open house, so that you can

send them reminder emails and any other necessary information. It also helps to reduce 'no-show' rates.

- **Have Some Refreshments Ready**: Nothing too expensive or elaborate; coffee and a few light snacks would do.
- **Be polite and ready to Answer Any Questions:** You don't want to appear as a difficult and unfriendly landlord to prospective tenants because the same way you are trying to avoid difficult tenants, is the same way that your tenants are trying to avoid difficult landlords. Therefore, you should try your best to be very friendly to every one of them, and answer their questions politely.

Hosting open houses helps to create excitement and competition around your property, and that helps you fill up your units faster. It also helps you save time especially if you don't want to be dealing with multiple showings for inspection, every now and then.

Next, we will be discussing how to manage and maintain the property.

MAINTAINING AND MANAGING YOUR PROPERTY

Multiple inspections are an essential part of the Section 8 Housing Voucher Program. You will regularly receive inspectors from the Housing Authority who always want to ensure that the housing units are in the right shape, and still conforms to the standards of the Housing Authority.

Properties that are not properly managed or fail to conform to the standards at any time may get kicked off the program.

So if you want to continue to make money as a Section 8 landlord, you must always ensure that your property is kept clean at all times, and properly managed.

We all know that maintaining a property where different people with different characters and maintenance cultures live is not a walk in the park. Some tenants are just naturally very rough and they will handle your property very roughly but since the Housing Authority always expects your property to be in good shape, it is up to you to devise strategies that would help you keep your property in good shape at all times. So how do you go about it? Here are some ideas:

Using a Property Manager- Questions to Ask

One of the most common strategies adopted by Section 8 landlords is the use of a property manager. The property manager is saddled with the responsibility of maintaining the property, amongst other things but before you go ahead and hire one, you need to decide if you really need one or not because property managers don't work for free, and if you must part with a significant portion of your rental income, you have to be sure that you really need to.

Duties of a Property Manager

Before you decide to hire a property manager or not, it is important to understand some of the duties of a property manager. The property manager will be responsible for relating with the tenants directly and then pass on any information you need to know to you. With a property manager, you can completely earn Section 8 income on a passive basis, where you set your checks or rent paid into your account every month, and you don't have to do anything else.

In this case, the property manager will be responsible for:

- Sourcing for new tenants, and filing vacant units
- Scheduling and hosting open house events
- Drafting and signing lease agreements
- Keeping track of rent payments and other financial issues and in some cases, the property manager is usually responsible for collecting the tenant's portion of the rent.
- Drafting and issuing all legal notices and correspondences.
- Carrying out criminal, financial and background checks on prospective tenants.

- Pre-screening and pre-qualification of tenants.
- Filing evictions
- Inspecting the property and scheduling all necessary maintenance repairs.

How Much Would You Have to Pay Property Managers?

Generally, property managers earn 10% of the monthly rent for each unit, and 50% of the first month's rent.

So if a new tenant moves in, and pays $1,000 per month for the unit he occupies, you have to pay the property manager $500 out of the $1,000 for the first month, and then 10% of $100 monthly rent, which is $100 every month.

These fees apply to every tenant/unit in the property. So, if there are 250 units in the property for instance, the agent would earn [$100 x 250 = $25,000] $25,000 per month.

However, in some cases, you may be able to negotiate with the property manager, and pay lesser fees especially for properties with many units.

Should You Use a Manager for Your Section 8 Property?

Managing your own Section 8 property yourself, is not a bad idea because at the end of the day, no one loves your property as much as you do.

You are also able to pocket more for yourself when you don't use a property manager but in spite of all these benefits, managing your property by yourself, is not always a good idea.

- If this is your first time of being a landlord, it is advisable for you to get a property manager. You may not know enough about the rules, laws, and guidelines guarding landlord-tenancy relations in your state, and this may lead to conflicts in the

future. You may also be exploited or frustrated by troublesome tenants.
- If you have a lot of other things that you do that keeps you busy, you should hire a property manager. Managing a Section 8 property is a full-time business and except you are retired, or not really engaged with many activities, you should hire a property manager.
- Lastly, if you want your property to be professionally maintained with necessary repairs and maintenance carried out immediately there is a need for it, or if you want to avoid tenants calling you up every time they have problems with their units, you shouldn't contemplate on hiring a property manager.

How to Choose the Best Property Manager

If you want to have complete peace of mind and earn, smooth passive income from your Section 8 property, you have to take out time to screen property managers before hiring them.

Some of the helpful factors you should consider include:

2. **The Number of Properties they are Handling**: A Property Manager who has too many properties to manage, might not be the most suitable option for you because they might not be able give your own property the deserved attention unless it is a management firm, with several managers to handle different properties. The fewer number of clients a property manager already has, the better for you.

3. **The Properties They Own**: Again, try to find out if this property manager owns any properties of their own. A property manager who has

properties of their own can better relate to a property investor's experiences and desires. They understand how you feel and what you want, and may be in the best position to manage your properties but there is always the issue of competition- how can you be sure that this manager would not choose to fill up his property vacancies over yours?

4. **What is their Property Inspection Routine Like?** You want a manager who can at least conduct weekly inspections and schedule maintenance repairs quickly so that your property stays ever ready for Housing Authority Inspections, and would always be in a good shape.

5. **How Attentive to Instructions Would They Be?** You don't want a property manager who is just out there doing his own thing without really paying attention to what you really want. You should be able to decipher this during interviews. When you are interviewing prospective property managers, watch out for those who try to finish off your sentences or cut you off during communication.

   Those are potential signs of a property manager who is likely to have bad listening skills.

6. **How Would they Handle Maintenance?** Often times, property managers take out a portion of the rent paid, and use it to resolve maintenance issues. You need a property manager that is willing to negotiate some of these fees and be ready to work with you to ensure that expenses do not surpass specific limits.

   You should also look for a manager who is ready to take less than 10% as management fees because

there are many managers who would be willing to take as low as 7% of the monthly rent as maintenance fees.
7. **Do they have Good Management Software**: A property manager with good software for managing tenants makes the entire process easy. It helps to also consider this when selecting your manager.
8. **Do they Have a Reporting System**: Lastly, you should find out whether the manager issues out regular reports to property managers. To make the business completely passive, you need to be given regular reports about what is going on with your property investment.

Let's take the discussion further where we will discuss how to deal with dirty tenants, as this might be part of what you are doing if you opt to manage the property by yourself.

Tips For Handling Dirty Tenants

Dirty tenants; every landlord has had them once, or will have them at some point.

The problem with dirty tenants is that they deface your property, and slowly reduce the market value. As a Section 8 Landlord, you must be proactive in dealing with dirty tenants because they can affect your ratings when the Housing Authority comes for its regular inspections. So how do you deal with dirty tenants? Here are some ideas on how to go about it:

1. **Learn How to Spot Dirty Tenants:** The best way to avoid dealing with dirty tenants is to learn how to spot them, and avoid renting your units to

them. You can just go right ahead and ask their former landlords about their levels of neatness, or interview them to understand their cleaning behaviors.

2. **Hire Cleaning Maids and Charge for It:** One way to prevent dirty tenants from damaging your property is to hire cleaners yourself and have them pay for it. The cleaners would be in charge of taking care of the building, and garbage disposal as well as any other thing that has to do with keeping the property clean.

3. **Be Tough on Cleanliness in Your Lease Agreement:** Your lease agreement must expressly state the terms of property use, the penalties that would come with disobeying such rules, and the tenant's cleaning responsibilities. If you don't do this, you may find yourself running your business at a loss because you may have to keep replacing items after each tenant vacates the unit and sometimes, the security deposits are not enough to cover for the damages.

Assuming that you've had lots of success after getting started as a Section 8 landlord, at some point, you will undoubtedly want to review your rent upwards. How should you go about it? The next part will discuss some ideas on how exactly to do this.

INCREASING YOUR RENT

Your ultimate goal in this business is to make as much money as you can and this means that sometimes, you may have to increase your rent to achieve this.

There are a few guidelines that you need to follow should you ever decide to increase your rent rates. First, you need to submit a request to your local section 8 office. This request will inform them of your desire to raise your rent. You will be asked to fill a form containing details about the current rent rates, the proposed increase, reason for the increase in rent rates, and when you plan to start charging the new rates.

The Housing Authority will then look into your request, and make their decision based on a number of factors:

- Verify that the rent you propose to start charging your section 8 tenants would not be higher than what you charge other tenants.
- Verify that your new rent rates would still be within fair market and payment standard rates.
- Verify that there is no fraudulent reason behind your decision to increase your rent rates.
- Verify that you've not increased your rent rates in

the last one year.

As soon as the Housing Authority makes these verifications, they will adjust the rent rates accordingly.

However, you must inform your tenants of your desire to increase rent rates, before you approach the Housing Authority. Tenants are responsible for paying a portion of their rent too, and some of them might choose to find a cheaper apartment rather than pay increased rental fees.

So both tenants and the Housing Authority should be equally carried along in the process, whenever you want to increase your rent rates.

So what about when you have to do the one thing that no landlord expects to do i.e. evict a tenant? Let's discuss that next.

EVICTING TENANTS AND TERMINATION OF ASSISTANCE TO THE TENANT

This is the part that scares many landlords away from the Section 8 housing program.

Most landlords are scared that they would be stuck with tenants that they cannot easily evict, should they fail to pay rents regularly, or fail to adhere to the terms of the lease.

The Housing Authority may also withdraw their assistance to a Section 8 tenant, and this means that you the landlord would have to figure out how to get your full rent rates from the tenant.

Their fears of such landlords are not unfounded though; it's not as easy to evict a section 8 tenant as it is to evict regular tenants, because the government is a part of Section 8 Tenancy contracts. However, it is not impossible to do so.

If you want to be able to evict your Section 8 tenant easily, and in a legally acceptable way, there are some rules and guidelines that you would have to follow. Let's briefly discuss that:

1. **Reasons for Eviction**: There are reasons for eviction that are acceptable under the law. Some

acceptable reasons for evicting Section 8 tenants include:
- Failure to pay rent
- Failure to pay for property damages caused by their own negligence or misuse of the property
- Fraudulent or criminal activity
- Harassment and disturbance of other neighbors
- Sub-letting a Section 8 apartment to other people
- Housing Squatters in a Section 8 apartment
- Illegal activities such as drug abuse, illegal possession of guns and firearms, and any other suspected criminal activities.
- Failure to adhere to the terms of the lease agreement.

You can cite any of the above reasons while evicting a tenant. Next, you have to send a pay or quit notice to the tenant

2. **Send a Pay or Quit Notice**: You have to send a notice to the tenant, asking them to either pay up outstanding rent, or quit the property within a number of days.

    To make your Section 8 eviction process work, you should give the tenants at least 30-90 days to quit. These are some of things that would be considered in court should you ever decide to file an eviction case. The court would want to be sure that you gave the tenant sufficient time to find an alternative apartment to live in.

3. **Notify the Housing Authority of Your Intention to Evict the Tenant**: Most states require that you inform the Housing Authority of your decision to evict the tenant. You should also give explicit reasons why you have decided to do

so, and the steps you have taken prior to this to avoid eviction. This is usually just for informational purposes and you can proceed with your eviction plan, whether the Housing Authority gives a nod or not.
4. **File an Unlawful Detainer with Your Local Court House**: After informing the Housing Authority of your decision, the next step is to file a complaint on unlawful detainer against the tenant with the local courthouse.

   The tenant will be summoned, and the eviction process will officially begin.

   When the eviction process commences or while it is still on, you cannot accept any rent payments from the tenants; otherwise, your case may result in unfavorable results, and you will be unable to evict the tenant.
5. **Evict**: As soon as the court gives you a go-ahead to evict the tenant, you can seek the help of law enforcement agents to help you achieve this because some evicted tenants may become hostile during this period, or fail to adhere to the rulings of the court.

Evicting a Section 8 tenant is not always easy but it can be achieved, as long as you follow the right procedures. Therefore, ensure to always play by the rules and the law will be on your side.

CONCLUSION

We have come to the end of the book. Thank you for reading and congratulations for reading until the end.

I hope you have found the book eye opening and practical enough for you to take action.

If you have non-section 8 tenants, as soon as you decide to put up your property for Section 8 rentals, you must ensure that the property is well taken care of.

Many non-section 8 tenants are often unimpressed with living side by side with Section 8 tenants because they believe that the property may become a 'slum'.

If you want non-section 8 tenants to still continue to rent your property alongside section 8 tenants, you must ensure that you conduct proper screening of potential tenants, and only rent your house to 'normal' people.

You should also ensure that the house is well taken care of at all times, so that people would find it difficult to tell the difference between your Section 8 property, and other properties around the area.

If you found the book valuable, can you recommend it to others? One way to do that is to post a review on Amazon.

Click here to leave a review for this book on Amazon!

Thank you and good luck!

Made in the USA
Columbia, SC
24 March 2018